Dear Jean
Many thanks for your wonderful
teaching this year. With love
from all at Artsplay Highland :) x

PRAISE FOR *INSIDE FOLK*

'Whether California dreamin' under giant redwood trees, busking in Paris or making music with worldwide celtic connections in Scotland, Liza Mulholland is a wonderful native guide to our national music, writing with great sensitivity and passion for her subject.

Her writing is also imbued with a kind of *Sehnsucht*, a German word meaning something more than longing – perhaps a longing for a collective unconscious which is in us all through the music she loves.

Here she encounters legends like Martyn Bennett, Karine Polwart, Phil Cunningham and Alasdair Fraser and places them all in the gathering stream of the great tradition of Scottish music and song.

Liza is a clear, engaging writer and a cultured guide who takes us from the poetic beauty of a Barra sunset to the crack and humour of musicians on the road across Europe, yet she finds time to lay flowers at Chopin's grave and immerse herself in the music of Mozart's home town.'

Billy Kay
Writer and broadcaster

'If music and arts are, as I believe, the best way to feed the soul, Liza Mulholland's beautiful writing about her musical adventures – with warmth, laughter, memories, knowledge, and a deep love of music - will help fill yours to the brim.'

Monica Neeling
Director, Artsplay Highland

D0185308

VOLUME 1

LIZA MULHOLLAND

INSIDE FOLK

VOLUME I

NOTES FROM A SCOTTISH MUSICIAN'S YEAR

FOREWORD BY SIMON THOUMIRE

First published in 2018

Metagama Productions Ltd
Reg. Johnston Carmichael
Clava House
Cradlehall Business Park
Inverness
IV2 5GH

British Library Cataloguing in Publication Data
A catalogue record for this book is available from the British Library

Paperback ISBN 978-0-9526669-2-9

The Inside Folk *series is dedicated to the memory of my parents, Bob and Peggy Mulholland, who provided the kindling for my musical life, and my grandfather, Jimmy Mulholland, who lit the fire.*

Contents

Foreword

It was a pleasure to be asked by Liza to write a foreword for her series of vignettes on life as a musician. Like many musicians I'm not much of a writer – I'm more of a doer. I get my creative satisfaction from the process of making things happen. I love the buzz of a new idea and then taking it to fruition and, while I obviously want the idea to succeed, I don't mind failing. I love seeing if an idea will work and thinking it through – and if it doesn't work, hopefully I can learn from it and pass on this experience to others.

The journey of balancing life as a musician and father or mother, wife or husband, can be a challenge. Creativity needs time and space – things that are rarer to come by the older you get. *Inside Folk* is a selection of such experiences which will resonate with many musicians. I look forward to everyone getting a chance to read them!

Simon Thoumire
Creative Director, Hands Up for Trad

Introduction

Over the years, hundreds of people have told me how they wished they had kept up their childhood piano or violin lessons, or the multitude of other instruments youngsters embark on, lamenting the loss of something they could now be enjoying. Too often, it is only much later in life we appreciate the worth and value of opportunities, and the rewards of perseverance and application.

I feel grateful, then, to my parents, not only for giving me the chance to learn piano as a young child, but also for somehow enabling lessons and practice to embed themselves into everyday life, as habit. Quitting music was never mentioned, so by the time I reached my final year of school and was paying for those lessons from my Saturday job wages, it still had not occurred to me that giving up was an option. For all this I am deeply thankful, for it has allowed me to enjoy a lifetime of playing music, with which have come numerous cherished, dear and close friendships, countless crazy adventures, lots of travel, a livelihood, many richly satisfying collaborations and projects, and an incredible amount of fun.

Although I was taught classical piano and brought up hearing a wide variety of music at home, my background – a large Glasgow-Irish family of musicians and singers on my father's side and the Gaelic song tradition of my mother's Isle of Lewis heritage – meant it was perhaps inevitable that I would feel the strongest pull towards folk music. Across the *Inside Folk* series, I will share a flavour of more than twenty-five years working in this genre. If you've ever pondered on the realities of life for a musician, I hope my books will offer an entertaining sense of the many joys and delights, trials and challenges, that we experience daily.

I use the word *folk* advisedly. I'm aware that, for some, it is still perhaps burdened by baggage associated with old-fashioned connotations, while the new cool vibe of the widely used and often-preferred term *trad* lifts our music clear of those stereotypes. However, it seems to me there are many overlapping areas with their own terminology – acoustic, nu-folk, neo-trad, alt-folk, roots – and so the term *folk* might offer an all-encompassing umbrella within which to explore, discuss and reminisce on some of the exciting, diverse and often innovative music we're fortunate to be surrounded by in Scotland.

In this first volume, *Notes from a Scottish musician's year*, I reflect on a number of elements integral to many musicians' lives, including performing, teaching, composing, travelling, listening, juggling children and work, and launching an album. The events, anecdotes and experiences do not represent one single year but are drawn from several, illustrating some of the common activities typically encountered and undertaken in that timeframe. My intention is to also attempt to set these pieces within a relevant context of wider Scottish culture and, at times, current affairs.

Several of these chapters began life in a column I wrote for an online Highland newspaper. The encouraging response made me realise readers were enjoying those brief insights into a musician's life and work, and thus inspired the idea for this *Inside Folk* series. While there is, particularly on the internet, more music writing than ever before in the form of gig, artiste and album reviews, I hope these volumes will help shine a little light on the everyday business of playing music in contemporary Scotland from a musician's standpoint.

To the many fellow musicians, singers and teachers, sound engineers, colleagues, writers and students I've had the pleasure of playing and working with, I owe a deep debt of gratitude, having learned greatly from all. Every musical relationship, collaboration and working partnership brings fresh insights, knowledge, creativity, skills, connections, tips and tricks to a musician's toolkit in what is, after all, a lifelong process of continual learning.

A piano arrived in our house one day when I was aged three, and I was captivated. Since then, music has been ever-present: a pervasive, enriching and enduring passion. I've leaned on it, relied on it, been freed by it, replenished by it. I'd be delighted if, in sharing a *blas beag** of my own love of music, even a few readers perhaps feel inclined to take up those instrument lessons where they left off in youth, or get along to a night-class, slow jam or weekend workshop. I adhere

---

* wee flavour/taste (Scottish Gaelic)

firmly to the conviction that you're never too old to learn and play music.

Liza Mulholland
June 2018

Celtic Connections

With another superb Celtic Connections drawn to a close, I find myself reflecting, in the festival's twenty-fifth anniversary year, on how profoundly the Scottish folk music scene has developed and blossomed in recent years. The renaissance has been so great across so many areas as to feel wholly transformational, and Celtic Connections both reflects and fuels this progress.

At the time of the inaugural festival in 1994 I lived in Glasgow, and I remember enjoying a late-night music session with friends in a crowded Hospitality Inn (there was no specific festival club that I recall), where excitement about this new folk entity was palpable. Although a tremendous success, with the *Glasgow Herald* newspaper proclaiming, 'It's big and it's brave', I don't think anyone attending that audacious initial venture could have imagined it would grow to become what it is today.

Now a world-renowned event lasting two and a half weeks, it features over 2,000 artistes in several hundred shows, selling over 130,000 tickets for events of all kinds – concert performances from intimate to epic, workshops, talks and New Voices Commissions – as well as delivering an extensive educational schools programme across Glasgow. Its reach and breadth has also spread to truly embrace international connections, fixing the festival securely in the calendar for musicians and music lovers, both home and abroad, as the heart-warming and replenishing tonic to see us through and beyond coldest, darkest January.

Although not playing at the festival myself this year, I had booked tickets well in advance for a concert I sensed would be one to hold close to the heart long after the event and cherish as a once-in-a-lifetime experience. Bothy Culture & Beyond proved exactly that. The show was a live theatrical arrangement of the second album by the supremely talented and groundbreaking Martyn Bennett, who died tragically young in 2005 at the age of thirty-three. A gifted player on many instruments, he embraced ancient and modern influences, composing music that defied categorisation. 'Celtic fusion' perhaps describes, somewhat imperfectly, his blending of the traditional Highland culture – poetry, story and dance, as well as music – in which he was deeply rooted, with the beats of the techno dance scene and the sounds and rhythms of middle-eastern influences.

I was fortunate to meet Martyn in 1998 during the Highland Festival, where I had a temporary job, not long after moving home to Inverness. Doing box office and artiste liaison for his show in my Ross-shire patch, I had the pleasure of ensuring that he was well looked-after and that everything around his gig went smoothly. I remember a quiet-spoken, gentle young man, pleasant and a little shy under his dreadlocks, but completely focussed on what he was there to do. He played a blinder, with any shyness banished as he stripped off to a bare torso and delivered a barnstorming performance of fiery piping and fiddling, with euphoric, syncopated rhythms and pounding, hypnotic beats. Watching him, it seemed he wasn't so much playing the music as channelling it – utterly at one with his instruments and somehow part of the music as it flowed, skirled and danced out.

Envisioning Bothy Culture for orchestra was tasked to the charismatic violinist, composer and conductor Greg Lawson, who had previously orchestrated Bennett's *Grit* album – and the result was breathtaking. Grand in scale and ambition, and complemented by a striking Cuillin ridge backdrop, spectacular lighting, beautifully edgy aerial artistry and the impressive stunt cycling of Danny MacAskill, it was a tour-de-force performance by Greg and The Grit Orchestra's eighty jazz, folk and classical musicians and their guest performers.

In Glasgow's massive SSE Hydro they joyously celebrated, with immense vigour, panache and heart, the work and life of a unique, free-thinking young man who demolished musical barriers and forged new cultural connections. To those of us in the audience absorbing the show, it was more than simply watching and listening; this evocation of the vision of Donald Shaw, Celtic Connections' artistic director, and Greg, felt glorious and at the same time deeply, achingly, poignant. It also felt more than a sum of its parts; there was an exciting sense that something much bigger was happening.

My friends and I almost danced back to the Holiday Inn, the now well-established post-show gathering place, where the bar was already filling up with musicians and concert-goers. As Grit players began arriving, hugs and warm congratulations abounded. Late-night tunes, catching up and getting the crack* with old friends are integral to the festival experience for musicians and, already high on Bothy Culture, we partied with gusto into the wee small hours.

Luxuriating in the delight of our one-night Celtic Connections fix, my thoughts dwelt the following day, as the train rolled quietly north through new-fallen snow, on the concept of legacy. I think it's reasonable to suggest musicians often feel as if we're part of a long, continuous, multi-thread string of music running through time and history – a sort of cultural continuum in which we are fortunate to participate and contribute. Many of us play instruments much older than ourselves, which have their own stories to tell, and we often play music that has been taught, or handed down orally, via a succession of players, singers and poets across many centuries.

Among most musician friends there is deep appreciation of who and what has gone before, and a sense of gratitude in that what we do is akin to bearing a musical baton – we are merely the ones in whose hands it resides for this ephemeral moment. The wonderful thing is, as Martyn's work amply demonstrates, the baton is never handed on identical to how we received it. Music is ever-evolving, shaped and renewed by circumstance, imagination, community, landscape,

---

*   fun, banter (Scots)

technology, the times we live in and their influences, so that traditional music's touchstones are continually realigned and re-oriented down through generations.

My mind wandered back to those who had been instrumental in the Scottish folk revival of the 1960s and 70s, including Martyn's mother, Margaret Bennett, Hamish Henderson and others who had laid the groundwork for the evening we had just experienced. Among the many influential and inspiring figures whose loss we feel keenly was a musician who injected that resurgence with a burst of exciting new creativity: Andy M Stewart. Born in Perthshire, Andy (who used his middle initial to differentiate himself from the White Heather Club entertainer of the same name), went to school with Dougie MacLean and Martin Hadden, where they formed a group called Puddock's Well. They all, at different times, went on to join the young Edinburgh band, Silly Wizard, with Andy taking on vocals, tenor banjo and tin whistle duties for the next fourteen years.

The prodigious virtuosity of teenage brothers Phil and Johnny Cunningham was marking Silly Wizard out as a groundbreaking new force on the folk scene, their supreme musicianship on fast fiery tunes, traditional and original, infusing the music with hugely exciting energy. With Andy's passionate and powerful interpretation of Scottish folk songs, and humorous warmth as onstage raconteur, this band of top-class musicians quickly gained widespread popularity during lengthy tours of the USA and Europe, going on to become one of the most influential folk groups of recent times.

It was Andy M Stewart's songwriting and delivery,

however, which cemented Silly Wizard's place in my heart. I recall, as a young teenager, my eldest sister returning from Glasgow University with albums, the like of which I'd not heard and whose very names sounded exciting – Moving Hearts, Planxty, Ossian – but it was when I heard Silly Wizard that something was truly fired in my brain. When I bought their LP, *Live in America*, it immediately became, and remains, one of my all-time favourite albums, and it was Andy's songs that I played and replayed until the vinyl was nearly worn through.

Andy had the gift of writing modern ballads that sounded traditional. Songs like 'Valley of Strathmore' felt as though they had always been there, his clear soft voice filling them with warm emotion. And then his comic genius surfaced in songs such as 'Ramblin' Rover', which I can vouch were sung with great relish at student parties across Glasgow's West End, and no doubt also much further afield. Unfortunately, I never got to see Silly Wizard play live before they broke up in 1988, but I was lucky enough to see Andy with Manus Lunny (now of Capercaillie), and it was, of course, a beautiful and unforgettable concert, where his personality shone as brightly as their music. Andy went on to record many more highly acclaimed albums, and continued to perform, write and tour until ill health overtook him. Failed spinal surgery rendered him paralysed from the chest down, and he sadly passed away after suffering a stroke and then pneumonia.

The influence of Silly Wizard cannot be overstated and, in recognition of this, the band were inducted into the Scottish Traditional Music Hall of Fame in 2012.

Andy's own contribution to the canon of folk song was immense; his became one of the defining voices of modern Scottish music, and his entrancing songs touched countless hearts and lives with their emotive lyrics, gorgeous melodies and warm humour.

The tributes that flooded in after his death, from so many of the folk world's leading lights, reflect the esteem in which he was held, and his far-reaching influence. I would guess that very few performers, young or old, at Celtic Connections – this year or any year – were not inspired, influenced or touched in some way by the magic of that particular Wizard.

Ten thousand people turning out to hear, cheer and experience a trad music concert in January 2018 is testament to how far things have come in a few short decades, and thanks, more specifically, to the rich and abundant legacy of those such as Martyn Bennett and Andy M Stewart, who ploughed a fresh, rare furrow in seasons past. It is, indeed, a precious inheritance.

Three hundred accordions free to good home

Chatting recently with my friend, Caroline Hunt, we meandered, after our usual exchange of news, on to the subject of her latest efforts to find a permanent home for her collection. Our conversation got me contemplating how it takes a very special kind of person to be a collector. Invariably organised, informed and highly focussed, their often-effusive passion is borne of enthusiasm for, and deep knowledge of, their specialism, and is reflected in what is usually an impressive understanding of the origins, craftsmanship and provenance of the objects.

Caroline is one such enthusiast, whose passion is not for small, easily stored and displayed items, such as stamps, thimbles or dolls, but accordions, and whose delight in all things squeezable has led to her acquiring over 300 of these wondrous instruments. With a desire for quality over quantity, she prefers not to duplicate items, resulting in her collection of antique accordions being one of the finest and most comprehensive in the world – possibly second only to Italy's famous Castel-fidardo Museum. As well as piano and button accordions, melodeons and concertinas, she has examples of bandoneons, flutinas, chemnitzers and harmoniflutes – as exotic-sounding as they are uniquely interesting.

I first met Caroline when she approached my then-husband Bruce MacGregor and I about the possibility of displaying some of her collection at our Bogbain Farm business, which was rapidly expanding on its windswept site overlooking Inverness. Both being musicians, we had been busy for some time developing the music side of our outdoor activities and events venue, with regular folk sessions, gigs and concerts, so the opportunity to establish an accordion museum fitted perfectly with our vision for Bogbain. We did not wait to be asked twice.

With her car packed full, Caroline made numerous deliveries with ever more fascinating instruments, building up a beautiful, shiny display of around sixty-five accordions, complete with information boards and books. Sourced from around the world, the selection included several rare items and illustrated the main developments and technological advances in the squeeze-box story, as well as examples highlighting the characteristics peculiar to particular craftsmen, factories and countries. With well-known accordion virtuoso Sandy Brechin doing the honours at a lively opening night, our Bogbain Accordion Museum was duly launched.

Despite playing accordion myself, I had little previous knowledge of its history, nor the diversity of specimens. Some were Heath-Robinson-type affairs with multiple keyboards, horns, bells and bows that would surely confound even the most ambidextrous, while others were pearly works of art, emblazoned with colour, enamel and diamante. I was intrigued when Caroline brought in a glass case containing a peculiar-looking free-reed instrument that was blown into; she explained that this type of Chinese Sheng was, in fact, the original ancestor of the accordion.

Not only was my own accordion knowledge greatly enhanced, but the collection proved a hit with our customers. The accordion is an attractive instrument and, despite a somewhat – and, I maintain, undeserved – chequered reputation, there is something irresistible in seeing dozens of them stacked up in all their colourful, glittering glory. I loved seeing visitors' eyes widen when first spotting the instruments and being drawn in wonder towards the sparkling spectacle of the display.

Our little museum was much-loved by tourists, many of whom travelled considerable distances to see the collection, as well as locals, fellow musicians and folk-lovers attending our music events and festivals. Sadly, it was not to last. In 2010 I found myself unable to continue in our business and Caroline was subsequently asked to take her accordions from Bogbain. She was back to square one.

Over the years she has had her accordions stacked floor to ceiling in her own house and, since removal from the farm, has stored many instruments in friends' lofts, garages and spare rooms. She is still seeking a suitable venue in which to house a permanent collection, and just as Castelfidardo attracts many thousands each year from all over the world, so Caroline's 300 accordions – in the right location with adequate space and facilities – have the potential to become a major Scottish visitor attraction.

In considering Caroline's resourcefulness and determination, I cannot but admire the contribution collectors have made to public life and the sum of human knowledge. From the curiosity cabinets of the sixteenth century to the Victorian heyday of collecting and classifying, individuals have been drawn to the process of gathering together objects of interest, and through protracted search, chance discovery and, sadly at times, imperialist plunder, have amassed exhibits with which to intrigue, amuse, teach, entertain and impress. Our museums today are testament to this, being filled with the diverse, intriguing and quixotic acquisitions of many of these tenacious, and usually wealthy, collectors and explorers.

If Caroline is representative of today's collectors then we are fortunate indeed, for she is someone with a sense of history and posterity, and who, through personal study and use of her own time and resources, has developed her initial interest in accordions into a substantial artistic legacy of great importance to Scotland. She is generously willing to make available to the public, for the benefit and enjoyment of all, a collection that is part of a wider cultural inheritance and vital to the story of our folk music and heritage

To twerk or not to twerk

For most of the seven years since we formed our band, Dorec-a-belle, we have had seven children aged up to twenty-two, which has, at times, posed considerable, diverse challenges. In addition, two of us are single mums, so simply doing the things that every band must do – practising, writing, gigging, business meetings and travelling – can become operations on a near-military scale. Recording our album, for example, over several days in Glasgow, involved highly detailed plans and intricate, logistical manoeuvres, pulling down troop movements and support back-up that would gladden the heart of any regiment commander. It also, perhaps, explains why we don't find too many thirty- or forty-something mums in touring bands.

However, none of us can imagine a life without playing music, and so we persevere. Our saxophone player and her husband have the biggest living room, and for several years we have gathered there to rehearse once a week, with kids in tow who would take themselves off to the nearby park or disappear upstairs to spend quality time with their mobile phones. When a new baby joined our troupe of offspring, feeding and nappy breaks became a novel feature of band rehearsals. We happily took this in our stride, along with the convenient opportunity for lots of extra tea and biscuit breaks for ourselves; if there are two things you learn through motherhood, it's compromise and making the best of, or finding solutions to, potentially problematic situations.

While still requiring battalion-style preparations, festivals are reasonably manageable because we can take our entourage with us. As most of the kids are now teenagers, being taken to exciting family-friendly festivals has turned acute embarrassment at mum playing in a band, into – if not quite kudos – at least unspoken acknowledgement of it being mildly beneficial. We had a significant breakthrough moment not long ago when one of our son's friends – we had lots of them camping with us; I'm not sure precisely how many as the head count kept changing – said of our performance, 'Dorec-a-belle are actually quite good!'. I could have sworn something approaching a hint of a smile twitched at the edges of our boys' mouths.

Youngsters can always be trusted to help keep feet on the ground, and this was thoroughly driven home for me at a concert support slot we did in an Inverness venue several years ago. With no babysitter available, I had to take my son with me and, demonstrating how interested he was in our music, he proceeded to get his school books out and do his maths homework in the front row. Try as I might to ignore this, maternal instinct kicked in and drew my eye towards him; it's somewhat distracting while playing, not to say tricky, trying to check his algebra upside down from the stage.

Incidentally, the task this wasn't made any easier by the fact the band we were supporting was The Magic Numbers.

Our children are now mostly old enough to be left happily at home and not dragged along to every rehearsal and gig, but for my teenage son there is a line in the sand over which mum must not step, under any circumstances. Chatting recently about the band, my lad said, 'Mum, you've got to promise something.'

'Yes … what's that?' I enquired.

'When you're onstage, promise me you'll never, ever … EVER …'

'What?!'

'Twerk!'

The notion that he thought I possess the physical strength and agility to execute some nifty Miley moves while wielding a weighty 120 bass accordion (or, indeed, *any* Miley moves, full-stop) is, with hindsight, quite touching. It made me realise that kids often view parents a little more generously than perhaps we view ourselves. When I'd picked myself up off the floor and my hilarity had finally subsided, I couldn't resist teasing, 'Hey, why not? Mum … twerking *(wiggle)* … with an accordion! What's not to like?'

He was not at all amused by even the faintest suggestion I might be serious, but on reflection I realised there could be mileage in this. If there's something I've learned over the last sixteen years, it's that bribery – or should I say reward – is a very handy addition to the essential parenting toolkit. The gist of it goes something like this, 'You know that gig I've got on Saturday … *(wiggle)* … see that untidy room of yours …?!'

Coughing, talking and muffin bells

'D' ye know 'Country Roads'?' slurred a fellow at a recent gig, stumbling in close to my face. Not only is it impossible to answer when singing, but it's also more than a little distracting to be interrupted mid-song by an inebriated punter who suddenly lurches forward, bangs into the mic stand and nearly knocks out your front teeth with the microphone. Steadying himself on the keyboard, causing it to wobble alarmingly, he leered in, waiting for an answer, eventually being hauled back by his friend and continuing to the toilet.

Pub gigs, or indeed any that are not 'sitting-listening' shows, where you share the same, sometimes intimate, space as the audience, can mean that such encounters are not unusual. Invariably, the proximity of the bar is a major factor, and the seasoned musician learns to take such interruptions in his or her stride and even laugh them off. I've witnessed overly gregarious dancers and party-goers knock over speakers, attempt to twang guitars (that are already being played), thump down a few piano keys in passing, and fall in among the drum kit as they lunge in to take a whack at a snare or cymbal. It's as if some latent desire to play music is unleashed by alcohol, propelling the now-uninhibited, would-be instrumentalist to the fore to 'have a go'.

The incident reinforced previous experience – that expectations of audience response and behaviour vary hugely depending on the type of venue and event. We don't realistically anticipate customers in pubs and bars will sit rapt through our performance, as they may not be there specifically to hear the band and might just want to chat with friends, although it is much appreciated when noise abates for at least the quieter numbers. But we don't expect them to ricochet in among us either. Physical interlopers are just one end of the interaction wedge, the other being the attentive audience who listen closely and respond with appreciative applause, or the enthused, dancing, cheering crowd who whole-heartedly get into the groove and love the music. What musician, after all, doesn't enjoy 'One more tune! One more tune!' chanted at them at the end of a great night?

Folk is a genre where there is far greater audience interaction than many other forms of music. Onstage banter, stories about the songs and tunes, and generally having the crack with the audience, have come to be very much part of Scottish musicians' shows, using humour to introduce even melancholy material with a playful approach. Many fans loyally attend every concert by their favourite artistes for the laughs, as much as for the excellent music; they know there will be lots of funny stories, witty quips, frivolity and belly laughs aplenty to take them flying home on a feel-good high.

Hilarious onstage impersonations by accordionist Phil Cunningham of fellow box player Fergie MacDonald, are so well loved, for example, to the point where Fergie in his own shows now tells stories about Phil's impersonations, and other musicians have extended the repertoire with their own affectionate takes and tales of the legendary Fergie.

Interaction such as this – laughing and singing along, responding to chat and even more lengthy involvement – not only sets a homely tone and atmosphere for the evening, but is heartwarmingly enjoyable for those on and off the stage. I recall the enchanting Karine Polwart conducting an achingly funny audience survey on the merits of different biscuits at a gig in Inverness's Hootananny venue. It must have lasted around ten minutes, but it was done with such natural wit and warmth that she had us not just laughing raucously with her but eating out of her hand for the remainder of the show.

Somewhere in the middle, however, lies a hinterland of etiquette that if navigated insensitively by audiences can not only disturb and spoil the flow of a performance but also deeply unsettle the musicians. Even in seated concert situations, where the assumption is that if customers have paid for tickets for a specific show then they want to listen to the music, I've witnessed utter disrespect for artistes as well as selfish disregard for other audience members; everything from shouting inappropriate comments, heckling and talking during the music, to disturbing others by being up and down continually to the bar and, later, toilets. And let's not mention the mobile phone and those who can't tear themselves from the grip of Facebook for even the duration of a concert, much to the annoyance of people seated behind, for whom blue scrolling light in their peripheral vision is a major distraction.

Prickly shame rises in me when I recall the Steve Earle concert in my home town a few years back. Being a long-time fan and not having seen him play live before, I was enormously excited about getting a sought-after ticket for his capacity show; I could not have been more disappointed. Not with Steve of course, who was superb, but with a small section of the audience who marred the evening for everyone. A gaggle of around fifteen or so drunks stood at the bar at the back of the hall throughout the concert, talking and laughing loudly, oblivious to appeals from fellow audience members, and the stage, to pipe down.

They had all presumably bought tickets, which weren't cheap, but I truly had no idea why they were there, as they paid no attention to the music and did not even notice when Steve, who was playing solo and didn't have the volume of a band to compete with this disrespectful lot, spoke directly to them. I fully expected him to down his guitar and leave the stage, but he played his full set, graciously and good-naturedly, despite the background noise. Why the bouncers did not deal with the situation, or close the bar, still perplexes me.

My friends and I left the venue that night embarrassed at being Invernessian and dejected at the thought that he most likely would never return to play our town. The gig would doubtless rank for him as a grim ordeal, so why would an artiste of global stature come back to a place where a portion of the audience spoiled it for everyone by lacking basic respect and failing to afford him the decency of listening to his music?

Sadly, competing noise and interruptions come in many forms, and they are neither a modern phenomenon nor confined to folk and roots genres. Virtuoso classical pianist Emil Saur – born in 1862 to a Scots mother in Hamburg – was reputedly impatient of interruptions, and if someone got up to leave the hall mid-recital he made a habit of stopping immediately, eyeing them sternly until gone, before taking to the keys again. It was reported in *Modern Musicians*, a compendium of the top musicians of the day, first published in 1913:

During a Saturday 'Pop' in London, he was compelled to interrupt his performance by the impertinent tinkling of a muffin bell in the street. He was just beginning Chopin's Fantasia in F minor, when the knell of the perambulating baker fell on his ear. What could he do but pause until the rival instrumentalist had passed out of range?

What indeed!

If it appears that I lay blame for all interruptions at the feet of audience and external elements, then let me rectify this by adding that we musicians are also guilty of occasionally sabotaging ourselves. Onstage disruptions might be technical – strings snapping, batteries failing, instrument malfunction – but they can also include wardrobe hitches and frailties of the flesh, such as calls of nature, hangovers, ill health and physical maladies that can manifest without warning.

At no time have I ever been a friend or supporter of Conservative policies, but when Prime Minister Theresa May was beset by a coughing fit during her party conference speech, I felt heart-sorry for her. That the media and some fellow Tories should round on her, as if coughing is a sign of weakness or ineptitude, baffled me. Who, after all, has not been momentarily hampered by a niggly throat, even if not during a crucial event? My empathy sprang from my own similar gruesome and disabling experience during a gig.

It was the early days of Dorec-a-belle and we were playing a cosy coffee house, and although the physical audience was correspondingly small, our intimate set was being beamed worldwide on Stageit. Years before Facebook and other live internet streaming platforms were developed, Stageit offered artistes an online 'venue' to play interactive and monetised live shows with a potentially global reach, tempting audiences with the chance of 'A front row seat to a backstage experience.' This was our first global adventure, and the cameras were set up to capture all the action.

All went well until midway through a song – I forget which one, amid the tracheal turmoil that ensued – when out of nowhere came a cough. I didn't have a sore throat, and I was singing only harmony vocals at the time, but something caught in my airway, setting me off rasping uncontrollably. Water was downed as I attempted to quietly disguise my discomfort, but the more I tried to clear my throat, the worse it got. I just could not stop coughing, and as it grew more hawking and violent I could hardly breathe, feeling as if my airways were being turned inside-out. With streaming eyes blinding my progress, I left the keyboard, blundered past the cameras to the little toilet on one side of us, where I loudly rent my lungs asunder.

It was fifteen minutes before the coughing finally subsided, my eyes cleared and I could breathe normally again, by which time our international debut was thoroughly ruined. I felt exhausted and wrung out by the physical havoc my body was subjected to, and although the girls in the band played and sang gamely and bravely on, I'm quite sure any viewers out there in the ether would have retreated to a place of ear safety by logging out of our show. Of all the things that can happen to mar or derail a performance, some simply cannot be foreseen; the antics of the tottering 'Country Roads' guy were nothing compared to my own self-induced *momentum horribilis*.

Fèisean treasure chest

I placed my accordion case on the floor beside me and asked the class if anyone knew what might be inside. A small, eager girl, her eyes wide with excitement, ventured, 'Is it a puppy?' It was a tiny country school with all twelve pupils in the room, and at once I felt the mean weight of the adult who must dash children's hopes. I opened the case, revealing the accordion, and a boy's hand shot up as he shouted in triumph, 'It's a banjo!'

Such are the delightful moments tutors have the privilege of experiencing, as we visit primary schools with the Youth Music Initiative (YMI), taking traditional music and Gaelic and Scots song to children across Scotland. A Scottish government-funded project, YMI is delivered in Inverness-shire and Ross-shire by Fèis Rois, and under the umbrella of Fèisean nan Gaidheal. Established in 1991, Fèisean nan Gaidheal is the independent association supporting an ever-increasing number of community-based Fèisean (Gaelic arts tuition festivals) as well as facilitating countless events and opportunities for young people, including workshops, ceilidh trails, drama projects, piping weekends and the wonderful Blas Festival.

The Fèis movement had its genesis on the Isle of Barra where, in the summer of 1981, something very special happened. While this small Hebridean jewel is of itself a uniquely special place, that year it was also pioneering. Local priest Father Colin MacInnes had the idea of holding a tuition festival in Gaelic song, music and dance for school-age children, to help promote the language and traditional culture. With the local community on board, and additional tutors and borrowed instruments ferried in, Fèis Bharraigh, the catalyst for an expansive cultural movement, was born.

I was fortunate to start teaching keyboard at Barra's Fèis in 1990. At that time, it was held over two weeks, for which we developed constitutions of steel to teach during the day and enjoy the nightly ceilidhs*, piping evenings, late-night sessions, dances (which often didn't get truly underway until nearly midnight), and after-dance parties. Some of us even found ourselves on the running track competing in the Barra Games, held in the middle weekend, providing much unexpected entertainment for our pupils.

It was an enormously satisfying and enriching experience; the youngsters were keen, I loved teaching and putting a small Fèis band together, and what could gladden the heart more than the simple delight of the sound of fiddle or clarsach† floating on a warm afternoon breeze, as children practised their tunes outside. The fun was endless; if I recall correctly, a certain young Glenfinnan

---

*   traditional Highland social visit/party
†   small Scottish harp (Scottish Gaelic)

fiddler arrived on a fishing boat for one night and ended up staying for a week, such was the crack.

So many unforgettable moments shine on in my mind's musical firmament. After one end-of-Fèis concert in Castlebay's old hall, everyone paraded down the main street to the pier, to wave off departing tutors and participants. I was staying for an extra day and got to witness the ferry pulling away in the evening sunshine, with Iain, piping tutor and youngest of those esteemed bagpipers and composers, the MacDonald brothers of Glenuig, on deck playing Runrig's beautiful tune, 'Cearcall a' Chuain'. The tranquillity of the setting, the ethereal 'Circle of the Ocean' wafting gently over the water, the clarity of a cloudless sky just beginning to lose its warmth as the sun lowered – I gazed, transfixed, as the boat glided gently through the silken surface of the bay. Already brimful of heady bonhomie from a fortnight spent in wonderful company, and immersed in work I was passionate about, it seemed as if elements of perfection had conjoined in those few transient minutes to evoke something almost spiritual. As the boat disappeared round the headland, the strains of Iain's pipes gradually faded, and we moved off back up the street in silence, with only the chatter and laughter of children rippling over our reverie.

The annual Fishermen's Mass is often held during Fèis week, when the people of Barra gather for the priest's blessing on those who go to sea and their vessels. This is another event I always felt privileged to attend, or experience, for it surely was an experience. One occasion, in the small Craigston Church on the west side of the island, was profoundly moving, with the community singing of the old Hebridean hymn 'Taladh Chriosda' forging a lump in my throat. Finding yourself in a place where people still sing – really sing – and where they know the words and sing as they have always done, heartily and joyously, can be an emotional shock – almost physical – such is its beauty. Perhaps I had a bad case of the romanticism of the outsider, but it seemed to me the swell of voices in the church that afternoon connected us back to something ancient and elemental. The melody of 'Christ Child's Lullaby' rose and then fell back in on itself, like waves surging on the shore just a stone's throw from the church; it was haunting and sublime.

In a book published to mark its twenty-fifth anniversary, Fèisean nan Gaidheal states:

Something that started off as a spark of inspiration of a parish priest … has grown from being a grassroots project to becoming a powerful artistic force which has played a key role in mainstreaming the Gaelic arts.

It is also helping fill the gap created by the changing dynamics of our modern lifestyles. Where music not so long ago was passed on, usually orally, within families and communities, this has altered dramatically, making the work of Fèisean – as well as instrumental tuition in schools – vital in keeping our culture alive. The fact that many of today's young tutors are products of the Fèis movement themselves, is affirmation that things have come full circle and are on a very healthy footing.

The impact of the Fèis network – which now comprises over forty tuition festivals and reaches around

13,000 young people – is evidenced in the thriving condition of the traditional music scene. Large numbers of ferociously talented youngsters are coming through in the MG ALBA Scots Trad Music Awards (Na Trads), the BBC Radio 2 Folk Awards, and BBC Radio Scotland's Young Traditional Musician Award, and are going on to become the new folk stars of festival and theatre circuits.

Not everyone embraces competition or aspires to be a top player; the simple joy, fun and satisfaction to be had in singing, playing, dancing and enjoying creativity, while learning from tradition-bearers, constitute something of the essence of it all. Karine Polwart, who has won many awards, most recently BBC Radio 2 Folk Awards' 2018 Folk Singer of The Year, commented, with her customary grace and wisdom, 'Competition isn't what fuels this music, is it? It's connection, and collaboration is at the heart of it.'

As well as fostering a nurturing sense of meaning, community and identity within our cultural traditions, it's well-known that participation in musical activities deeply enriches lives and enhances our sense of well-being. Thankfully, Fèisean are not confined to youngsters. Some are open to adults too, and Fèis Rois Inbhich – an adult Fèis weekend – is one such, held annually in Ullapool, which enables older participants to enjoy similar opportunities. Indeed, it has changed lives, with several students and tutors meeting their future spouse at the Fèis (including myself in 1995). It's a superb event, with ever-increasing numbers turning up to learn or improve on an instrument, try step dancing or Gaelic song, proving that you're never too old to enjoy music and attempt something new.

In an essay for the *Sunday Herald* newspaper in 2012, Donald Shaw of Celtic Connections noted the part played by Fèisean in the blossoming of our folk heritage:

The source of this new-found confidence and appreciation of our own country's traditional music can be traced, at least in part, to work at a grassroots level in schools and workshops across Scotland, and in particular the Fèisean movement. This movement has flourished because of the constant stream of passion and experience passed on by a community of mentors who understand the power of music to build a community and satisfy the soul.

A quotation attributed to one Dr Maya V. Patel states, 'The soul of a country is in its folk music. The country that has abandoned its folk music to commerce deserves a Coca-Cola wake.' While we have organisations like Fèisean nan Gaidheal continuing to develop the important work of the last few decades, Scotland's soul is surely safe.

I am reminded of another recent heart-warming incident as I made my way to the classroom in a local primary school. It was a dress-down day, and as I trundled my accordion trolley along the corridor a small boy in pirate costume pressed himself against the wall to let me pass. His eyes fixed on my ancient, black wooden accordion case as I wheeled it carefully by his toes, his plastic cutlass primed for action.

'Treasure!' he murmured, gazing after the box as I continued past. I like to think that, in a way, he was right.

All in a day's work

Madonna's onstage fall at the Brit Awards in 2015 demonstrated, all too painfully, one of the occupational hazards awaiting the performing musician. But there are many more, even for those of us not cavorting around in capes and high heels, surrounded by troupes of dancers in intricately choreographed routines.

Not so long ago I developed a debilitating condition in the Achilles area of my left foot; not only was it swollen and sore, but as it got worse I found I couldn't place my foot flat on the ground and so ended up walking with a limp. This led to me progressively over-compensating with my right leg, which, in turn, caused sore hips and back pain, leaving me hirpling around like a very old woman, having to cling to the banister to manoeuvre myself sideways down stairs.

If this conjures up a particularly unflattering vision, be assured it was exactly that. And the cause of all this misery? Tapping my foot too hard on the floor when I play and at times, I confess, stamping. When I was learning classical piano as a child, under no circumstances was I allowed to tap my foot in time to the music, but in the much more relaxed folk world I developed the ubiquitous foot-tapping habit when playing. It became not only automatic but fervent, to the point of injury.

Diagnosed by the physiotherapist as tendinopathy, it was months of exercises and a pair of particularly unattractive, sensible sandals later, before it subsided. My affected Achilles tendon has not fully healed, and I now must consciously, and constantly, monitor those wayward feet of mine when I'm playing.

Were health and safety inspectors to do risk assessments for musicians, they might also highlight: repetitive strain injury; lock jaw; cubital, carpal and tarsal tunnel syndromes; tendinitis; tendinosis; tinnitus; bursitis; dermatitis; de Quervain's syndrome; Garrod's pads; myofascial pain disorder; ganglions (caused by tight straps – not S&M, but the accordion variety); temporomandibular joint disorder; and last, but by no means least, trigger thumb.

These medical textbook conditions conjure for me visions of the gothic and grotesque; a dusty anatomy museum perhaps, glinting with ancient specimen jars, in which float coiled and convoluted rubber-yellow scraps of succumbed musician. Also included might be the slightly less formal, but equally colourful, fiddler's neck, bagpiper's fungus (nothing to do with feet but a lung disease caused by inhaling fungal spores from inside the pipe bag), flautist's chin, horn player's palsy, harpist's cramp, cellist's dermatitis, trumpeter's lip, singer's nodules, burst eardrums, mashed lips, and a host of other afflictions, including shoulder, neck and back injuries.

Pipers appear to have an especially troublesome time. Old friend and top piper Donald McBride recently had surgery for Dupuytren's Contracture, sometimes called Viking Disease, from over-use of the 'pinky' finger of his right hand in playing *birls* (musical ornamentation). Two long, intensive days of teaching and playing had caused the tendon from his little finger to contract, raising several nodules on his palm and disabling the digit in question. The temporary loss of use of even one finger is not just painful and inconvenient for a piper during the recovery period but can also mean loss of income and livelihood. Those pesky birls!

Those are some of the basics, but then there are all the random threats to life and limb lurking in the stage wings. When pigeon excreta, from a bird enjoying (or maybe not) a Kings of Leon performance from its perch high up in the rafters, landed in the mouth of the bassist, the St Louis concert was abandoned as 'Too unsanitary to continue'. While not pleasant, throwing in the towel three songs into their show might be regarded as light-weight by the hardy breed of rockers that includes Otto Schimmelpenninck – bassist (is it something about bass players?) with Dutch metal band, Delain – whose testicle was ruptured by an onstage confetti cannon, but who soldiered on and finished the concert despite immense pain and discomfort. The indestructible Keith Richards was electrocuted and knocked unconscious, while Patti Smith broke her back tripping on a stage monitor and falling fourteen feet.

Sometimes enthusiasm itself is enough to fell the passionate musician; one well-known and greatly re-vered Scottish fiddler was unaware that, as his playing grew more vigorous, he was causing the legs of his chair to shuffle in tiny increments towards the edge of the stage. The resulting ultimate indignity was later immortalised in the rollicking fiddle tune, 'Farquhar's Rocking Chair', by Bruce MacGregor on his *Loch Ness* album.

And if the audience gets over-exuberant? Outcomes vary, but they can often pose danger to life and limb; Frank Zappa escaped death when a fan fired a flare gun at the ceiling during a Swiss show and burned the venue to the ground. However, he wasn't so lucky on another occasion when he sustained multiple injuries after an audience member sneaked onstage and pushed him into the concrete orchestra pit. If you are Tom Jones then all you risk having flung at you is female underwear, but what are *fans* thinking when they chuck bottles, lollipops (one of these got lodged in David Bowie's eye socket), urine bombs, deckchairs (50 Cent took the hint and ended his show at that point), and coins? Occasionally, musicians suffer freak accidents and pay the ultimate price. Composer and orchestral conductor Jean Baptiste Lully's conducting staff pierced his foot during a performance of his Te Deum in 1687 – bad enough, but he later developed gangrene and died.

Even if we manage to dodge projectiles, avoid injury, evade personal attack and sidestep serious medical ailments, there are still a host of 'biggies' stalking musicians everywhere: alcoholism, stress-related depression, performance anxiety, substance abuse and penury. All lie in wait for the unsuspecting troubadour.

So why, you may ask, do we do it? Well, health,

personal safety, financial security, sanity and longevity may well be at risk for any gigging musician, but what is certainly guaranteed is the most fun, creative satisfaction and joy imaginable. And, as the plucky Madonna so conclusively illustrated, the show must go on.

Solace for the soul in times of trauma

When I'm working from home – dealing with emails, planning lessons or tackling the edifice of admin that now seems to blight most musicians' lives – I often have BBC Radio 4's music programmes on in the background. Consistently intelligent and full of interest, series such as *Behind The Scenes*, *Soul Music* and *Tales From The Stave* have touched and taught me much. One recent programme, on the power of music to affect us and offer comfort and succour at difficult times in our lives, resonated acutely.

Several years ago, my life was changed forever when personal events turned my world upside down, leaving me almost paralysed with shock and feeling like I had been run down by a ship. 'Devastated' is a word so overused in modern parlance as to render its meaning severely blunted, but in this case the sharp blade of destruction did indeed lay waste. So, how do you claw your way back to some semblance of emotional and mental equilibrium, when everything is changed in an instant? When you can't eat or sleep, and that ship's thick mooring rope remains stubbornly knotted in your stomach for months? How to cope with the demands of everyday life, work and children when you're stumbling around in a daze?

There are no quick fixes, and trauma on any scale produces a fall-out of shock and stress that may require medical or psychological intervention. We hear of horror and tragedy so great that we are left wondering how on earth those involved can ever recover from such unimaginable grief. Whether in distant lands or tragic events closer to home, we realise that, as a chaplain supporting victims in one recent, very public, tragedy concluded, sometimes there are no words of comfort; there is simply nothing that can be said to ease the pain.

Regardless of the nature of the personal crisis, it can have a profound, overwhelming impact on our physical health just as much as on our psychological well-being. I was fortunate to have the love and support of many good friends – whether at my side on long winter walks and talking over endless cups of tea at my kitchen table. Their wise words assured me that time, the great healer, would gradually bring some ease, and helped me find ways through those interminable early days. And I tried music.

To my dismay, I found that I couldn't play. Going to the piano, nothing would come. Desolation had robbed me of inclination, interior joy, the creative spark or whatever it is that drives musicians to play. Singing was also impossible; not only did my vocal cords feel melded together in a solid throaty lump, but the urge to sing was stone dead.

Naturally, it is the emotional resonance of music which makes it the art form that touches people, probably more than any other. In troubled times it allows us to cry, wallow in our loss or heartbreak, feel sadness and nostalgia to our core, to reflect and be comforted. I only needed to hear, in passing, a fragment of gentle tune or sad song on the radio, for tears to well.

Singing and playing music takes that emotional outlet to an even higher level. For the thousands on the streets of Paris commemorating those who died in the Charlie Hebdo killings, the singing of 'La Marseillaise' was not only symbolic but would also have brought a measure of solace: a remembered resilience, a shared balm soothing the pain. Although I speculated that my inability to play would be temporary, I felt bereft – something I had always taken for granted, part of my identity, had just evaporated.

Then one night, around six months later, something happened. With my son in bed, I sat noodling half-heartedly at the piano. Suddenly, a little chord progression presented itself, triggering some words, a phrase, a melody, and before I knew it, a song was tumbling out. 'On the Road' was not a diatribe of anger but a gentle ballad, a contemplative reflection on what life can throw at us. The floodgates had opened, and if my mojo wasn't quite back and jigging delightedly at least it was in the vicinity.

In his 2013 BBC Reith Lectures on art, Grayson Perry likens artistic creation to a personal shed: a private place into which he can withdraw, hide and immerse himself. Music is the same. Playing and writing allows you to lose yourself, becoming simply a conduit for the strange, mercurial phenomenon that is music; it is utterly absorbing, therapeutic and immensely satisfying.

As months lurched by, more songs unravelled themselves to me and gradually the sheer joy and love of a good tune kicked in, much to my relief. I knew some progress had been made when I found myself and my son belting out 'Price Tag' along with Jessie J, as we drove to school. There's nothing like unselfconscious, full-volume car-singing to lift the spirits on a Monday morning.

When Dorec-a-belle formed, another restorative musical adventure began – one which has brought ever-increasing satisfaction and delight, not to mention mutual support and fraternity. Building on the essentials of good strong songs, the musical textures, colours and harmonies that have come to characterise our sound are a joy to be part of. A beautiful song that has become a staple in our set list is one written by the late Ian Frew, father of our guitarist, Maryann. 'Don't Give Up' resonates to such a degree that each time we perform it I am lost in its words and melody – its message of hope overcoming pain and loss – as if it was meant directly for me.

The ability of music to take you outside of yourself is like the touch of a healing hand, or an out-of-body experience without the use of drugs. David Byrne of Talking Heads, states in his book, *How Music Works*:

> *Music can get us through difficult patches in our lives by changing not only how we feel about ourselves but also how we feel about everything outside ourselves. It's powerful stuff.*

How right he is.

A few of my favourite things

Schools had closed, youngsters were universally elated as the freedom of long summer holidays beckoned, and the sun was at last shining. This alone was enough to set me whistling perkily, but I was more than usually excited about the holidays. Although playing the main stage of our local Belladrum Tartan Heart Festival with Dorec-a-belle was enough to make this musician's summer complete, on top of that I would be attending a week-long training course for my early years' music work with Artsplay Highland.

While always highly enjoyable, useful and enriching in my development as a youth music practitioner, training does not necessarily have me automatically salivating at the prospect, but when it's a trip with my lovely colleagues to Salzburg it's somewhat different. An opportunity to attend an international summer school at Austria's Universität Mozarteum – the world-famous academy of music and drama – to study the methodology, theory and practice of music teaching, as devised by the eminent Carl Orff? You'll understand why there were cartwheels round the garden!

Salzburg is the birthplace of Mozart, and for a classically trained musician, or indeed any music lover, the opportunity to visit his home and walk in his footsteps around the city, would, I think, be grasped with both hands. Most fans, be it of a composer, writer, pop or film star, feel a strong connection to their hero or heroine by being in their home, almost breathing the same air, in a way that no other avenue of admiration or adulation allows. To stand in the very room in which they were born or raised, view objects which would have been familiar to them in childhood, gaze on the detail of their family surroundings, and relish the knowledge that possibly not much had changed – and therefore the eyes of genius had perhaps viewed the same scene – is exhilarating.

To see the desk at which the writer worked, or the instrument from which was wrought music of brilliance, is special beyond words and seems to strike a universal chord across humanity. In a strange way, it's perhaps not so far removed from how religious reliquaries containing ancient shreds or shards of saint or martyr are imbued with unique significance and potency for the devout. To behold the genuine article – or if extremely lucky, touch it – allows the concertina of time to squeeze the years and centuries down to nothing, ushering in living history.

Paying homage at a grave brings you closer still to your idol. Gigging in Paris with a Glasgow band many years ago, I made sure to visit the legendary Père Lachaise Cemetery. But while the grave of The Doors'

Jim Morrison was the main attraction for dozens of fellow twenty-somethings – many of whom spent hours there, hanging out, smoking, drinking and laying flowers in silent respect – my goal was to seek out the resting places of several slightly less modern musicians whose work I loved: Frederic Chopin, Edith Piaf and Maria Callas. I enjoyed the added benefit of finding, by accident, Oscar Wilde's tomb, but it was at Chopin's feet that I laid my small floral posy, and I recall the intense sensation of touching the stone of his grave bringing me nearer him.

The closest I'd previously been to Mozart was in Prague. I was fortunate to be there on holiday when his opera *Don Giovanni* was performed at the Estates Theatre. To see this work in the theatre where it was originally premiered and conducted by Mozart himself in 1787 was nothing short of thrilling; perhaps my imagination was playing tricks, but I was certain I felt ghosts of another time in that magnificent place.

Those who walked before us were felt throughout Salzburg's ancient centre, the worn stones and cobbles of every lane, street and civic space witness to centuries of stories unfolding and lives played out. Droves of tourists snapped selfies and hoovered up the Mozart trinkets, T-shirts and chocolates adorning windows of little huddled shops: modernity amid antiquity. Those same crowds filed through both homes of the Mozart family – we all had the same idea – and so the experience, although fascinating, was unfortunately not so much quiet, reflective contemplation as conveyor-belt processing of bodies from room to room. In the height of summer, it was to be expected.

From the achievements of a child prodigy to a pedagogy whose central theme and aims are to release, encourage and build creativity in all children, through an integrated approach of instrumental music, song, movement, dance, speech and play. The artistic legacy of this methodology, devised and practised by Carl Orff, perhaps more popularly known for works such as *Carmina Burana*, has been hugely influential in music education and, nearly a century on, has spread globally.

The summer school was the most widely multi-cultural event I have ever attended. As well as our small Highland contingent, there were over 100 music educators from around the world – as far away as the USA, Brazil and Argentina in one direction, and Iran, Georgia and China in the other. The lecturers and tutors, likewise, hailed from numerous countries, and it was a fascinating privilege to learn from the teachings of diverse cultures as they used the folk song and dance of their own traditions to illustrate Orff methodology, impart concepts and equip us with musical tools to engage and develop children's creativity.

They invited us out of our comfort zones and, in the safety of the supportive gathering of new friends, we tentatively ventured into some uncharted territories, including, for me, the untried and unfamiliar artform of contemporary dance. While I love dancing, be it whirling a Highland Schottische at a ceilidh or strutting my stuff in a club, I regret to say my lack of supple joints and non-existent agility mark the contemporary form as very much a work in progress. I would say 'watch this space', but most probably it will remain thus – I'm always happy to throw shapes in the air but not quite so much on the floor.

The trip was by no means a holiday, with a full timetable of classes over six days and additional nightly workshops and seminars. One of my highlights was the 'ceilidh' evening where each country introduced a flavour of their folk culture to fellow participants. In a large hall bursting with musicians and teachers, each little group shared their songs and dances; the range and beauty of folk arts from this 'united nations' gathering was truly glorious. There were so many of us, and everyone was so enthusiastic about sharing, that it spilled over into the following evening and lots of laughs were had as we joined in, attempting unfamiliar languages and dances.

In representing Scotland, we packed as much as possible into our fifteen minutes; I gave a whistle-stop introduction, touching on the post-Culloden destruction of traditional instruments and persecution of Gaelic and Scots language, through to the modern revival of interest and confidence. It being not long after the independence referendum, I couldn't resist mentioning how the engagement around that debate had led to an uplifting burgeoning of music, song and creativity. Eilidh Mackenzie then taught and led a Gaelic waulking* song, as Artsplay director Monica Neeling and Emily Scott organised students around the huge piece of 'tweed' on the floor. It was tremendous fun and, although some students looked a little bemused by the waulking actions, we think they enjoyed their wee taste of this old Scottish tradition.

---

* the traditional process of shrinking tweed, while sitting around a table, thumping it down and passing from hand to hand, accompanied by rhythmic Gaelic song.

What stood out for me, though, was the Georgian contribution. Despite being the sole representative of his country, this ambitious chap patiently taught us a traditional Georgian song of multiple, complex harmonies. At one point I had to stop singing just to listen, so stunningly gorgeous was the result: ethereal and transcendent in its cantatory beauty, voices interweaving around each other with strange, sometimes dissonant, harmony. It was stunning.

As we explored the historic heart of Salzburg on our free afternoon, I marvelled at the abundance and magnificence of the music which has rung through its churches, streets, schools, homes and halls over many centuries, even in its parks. *The Sound of Music* was filmed in the city, and as a much-loved childhood movie and one whose songs my sisters and I sang lustily around the house for years – we even had the LP – it retains a special, nostalgic place in my heart.

I often ponder on the bizarre fact that music is simply a disturbance of the air at different frequencies and, this being so, could musical vibrations from long ago still be bouncing around, akin to the light from distant stars taking us back in time? As I made my pilgrimage to the gardens where Maria led the Von Trapp children in those delightfully memorable songs, I couldn't help but listen out for strains of ghostly melodies. Whether it be long-lost vibrations of Mozart's sonatas or 'Doe A Deer' I wouldn't care; all were meaningful landmarks on this visitor's musical journey.

California dreaming: five Scottish fiddlers have fun in a trunk

There are rare folk musicians who achieve revered, almost iconic, status for generations of players and music lovers. This can be for many reasons, including virtuosity, style, interpretation, superb composition and personality, but usually also because in some way they have broken new ground, or opened fresh doors, along the wide and cherished corridor of tradition. Seeing fiddle player and composer Alasdair Fraser perform again reminded me of why he has been so admired, and such an important influence, over three decades. It also brought rollicking back the incredibly fun and crazy week spent at his fiddle school in the hills above Silicon Valley in California.

It was 1997, and Bruce and I had just seen Alasdair play in Inverness's beautiful Balnain House. Bruce had introduced me to Fraser's music two years earlier and, as a fiddle novice, I was in awe of his infectious tunes, his heartfelt and sympathetic interpretation of Gaelic song and his mastery of the instrument. We both came away from the concert enormously inspired, not just by the sheer beauty and emotional depth of his playing, his tonal quality and compositions, but by the man himself – his energy and the boundless musical possibilities he enthused about. His Californian fiddle camp sounded too good to miss.

We duly signed up, with Bruce undertaking to record material while there for a feature programme for BBC Radio Scotland. The adventure grew ever more appealing when we discovered three musician friends also intended to go, and so arrangements were duly made to rendezvous at Glasgow airport. After our fiddles and cases were closely inspected, and security satisfied we were neither gun runners nor drug mules, we boarded and settled in for two long flights to America's west coast.

Our little Scottish cohort of five fiddlers was met at San José by a yellow school bus, and as we wound our way up through forested hills and into the redwood groves of Boulder Creek, the first sight of the great trees was breathtaking. Arriving at camp to find wooden lodges and cabins nestled around the ankles of these giants rendered us speechless; while we appreciated the remnants of our own Caledonian Forest back home in Scotland as strikingly majestic, nothing had prepared us for this.

John Steinbeck, in *Travels with Charley*, his 1962 journey of rediscovery across the United States, describes these titans of his native California as, 'ambassadors from another time'. Emphasising that no one had yet managed to adequately portray the *Sequoiadendron giganteum* in words, art or photography, he goes on to observe, 'There is a cathedral hush here [...] a remote and cloistered feeling. A stunning memory of what the world was like once, long ago.'

Perhaps the otherworldliness of these ancient trees rubbed off on us, or maybe we should have guessed from the camp name – Valley of the Moon – that strange things might happen in this place. Either way, it was to be no ordinary week. Playing music in the quiet shade and warm scent of the redwoods felt magical – almost as if those living, breathing beings were listening. A calming peace settled on us all and, with wonder and respect, we offered up our weave of notes, dancing gently upwards to be lost in the high canopy, and in return were nourished by the presence of the mighty ones.

If this sounds a little hippy-like, it's because a sprinkle of that rubbed off on us, too. Of the 200 students, the majority were American, some were Canadian and then there were us; we did try to fit in, but going with the Californian flow didn't always come easily. On our second evening, I was queueing for communal dinner in the main lodge when I suddenly felt hands rubbing my back. I instantly bristled and turned (probably scowling) to find a lean, greying, ponytailed man in flip-flops smiling at me.

'Gee, are you always this tense?' he asked, as he worked his seasoned fingers on my rigid shoulders. I *wanted* to say, 'No, only when a total stranger decides to give me a massage while I'm waiting for my tea, and, by the way, I don't recommend you try this in Glasgow.'

But I shrank under the accusation – I was indeed an uptight Scot – and managed only a pathetic, quavering whimper.

As the queue edged all-too-slowly along, he gave it laldy,* kneading and pummelling at my recalcitrant Highland back. My stiff embarrassment festered into panic as I wondered what on earth I should do. What was the etiquette? Was I meant to return the favour, spin around, flick his ponytail to one side and start on him? Thankfully, my masseur gave me up as a lost cause as the veggie lasagne loomed into view, but my first stop, post-dinner and in some haste, was the bar for several swift, healing beverages.

There are no two ways about it, an honesty bar can be a wolf in sheep's clothing. The anonymous pay-as-you-go type is painless and to be welcomed, but at Valley of the Moon there was a large board on which, underneath your name, you noted down the drinks you'd taken. It's with some regret that I recall we did, rather heartily, live up to the Scottish stereotype, for which we felt more than a little ashamed. While most folk listed a dozen or so beers by the end of the week, we Scots had not only reached the bottom of the board but were halfway down a new column.

We stayed up late, trailed last into class in the morning – most students were seated long before the tutor arrived, such was the determination to secure a spot in the front row – and partied hardest. When it came to theme night, where cabins hosted each other in a sort of moveable, nocturnal ceilidh, we set up shop inside a vast remnant of tree trunk. Almost the size of a small

---

*   vigour/energy (Scots)

apartment, this ancient relic was hollow and burned out – perhaps hit by prehistoric lightning – and, complete with fiddles and keyboard, we kicked off our party.

As darkness fell, trad became trance, with a side helping of funk, and with just a few torches and lanterns to light our ceilidh house, more and more friends piled in until the redwood ruin was a heaving, howling mass of humanity and music. A deep primeval instinct was awakened in us as Chris pounded out a beat and menacing bass chords on his keyboard, fiddles swirled mesmerising patterns all around and tribal chants and shrieks shot forth as we pulsed new life into this ghostly great-grandfather of trees. Lubricated just a little by that honesty bar, we communed with the ancients, bonded with the universe and at last our Scots cringe was set free and let fly off into the night.

What a week. The classes were fabulous, tutors – including Martin Hayes, Bruce Molsky and Barbara MacDonald Magone – superb, and the setting utterly awe-inspiring. Alasdair Fraser himself was understandably adored by the students; his holistic ideas on music as part of life's tapestry, and emphasis on how the roots of our folk tunes are so inextricably linked with dance, chimed with the open-minded gathering. Here was a master of the fiddle, who was not just teaching tunes but also history, culture in the widest sense and, indeed, elements of philosophy.

Bruce captured the spirit of the school in his programme, *Valley of the Moon*, for Radio Scotland, and I grew in confidence on the fiddle and in piano accompaniment, as well as learning much about life. Whether in the company of a colossus of the fiddle like Fraser, or giants of the natural world, it's possible to feel very small – insignificant even. But, depending on how you look at it, that can be both a comfort and a release. The cycle of life goes on and we are all standing on the shoulders of our forebears, musically or otherwise. As for the *funk trunk*, I like to think music lingers yet among its blackened, primordial roots; come to think of it, I'm not sure some folk ever did make it out of there.

Festival frolics from toddler to teenager

As musicians, I think we all harbour hopes that our children might also show an interest and participate in music. While our own knowledge and experience of the challenges of making a sustainable living from it may also serve to try and guide our offspring away from the notion of playing professionally, it is natural that the wondrous thing we've had the privilege of enjoying throughout our lives, and which has brought us so much fulfilment and pleasure, we would also wish for them.

Being the son of two musicians, our baby was inevitably exposed to lots of music from the start. *In utero* he was close-up and personal with my accordion (whether he liked it or not), often heard his parents duet on fiddle and piano, and was very much present during our mini-tour of several English folk clubs when I was quite heavily pregnant. He was also fortunate to be surrounded, as a thirty-two-week foetus in October 2001, by the magnificent sonic riches of over

120 fiddlers in full swing at our inaugural Blazin' In Beauly music school.

What infants hear in the womb is now found by scientists to be much more acute than previously thought, and it is also deemed highly significant to their future development. Recognition of parental voice aids bonding, and hearing a wide range of sounds, including music and song, stimulates brain development and cognitive function. The song sung by a mother, slightly muffled from within the warm, watery confines of her belly, will also relax and settle her baby in the outside world, just as a lively tune that excites the infant in the womb will elicit similar wriggling and kicking of legs in enjoyment and recognition after birth.

I suppose, then, it was no surprise that our wee fellow loved nothing better than to sit on my knee at the piano and thump his little hands down on the keys. The delight on his face, accompanied by excited gurgles and yelps as he realised it was him making the sounds, were enough to fill my heart to overflowing. As months went by, he ceased thumping – discovering instead that if he used one pointing finger the sound was clearer and more interesting to him, and what's more he could then choose which single key to press down. I noted this as something of a marker in the beginning of our wee lad's musical appreciation.

His toddler days were filled with our own music and that of friends and colleagues – mainly Blazin' Fiddles, who often rehearsed in our living room – and he enjoyed scampering around during the regular folk sessions and gigs we hosted at our Bogbain Farm venue. I was also keen, however, that he be exposed to a variety of music, and so determined, where practical, to take him to festivals and concerts.

Our first festival outing was to nearby Belladrum the year after it started. My first time camping alone with my three-year old, I was realistic enough to guess that I probably wouldn't get to see many of my chosen bands – indeed I spent most of the time simply shadowing him – but I hadn't quite bargained for the logistics of embarking on this expedition alone.

Full of wholesome intentions to have a genuine camping adventure, I had taken the works: a stove, ridiculous amounts of food, several changes of clothes for all weathers and even – don't ask me why – a pile of toys. After several trips back and forth from the car with all this baggage and getting the tent set up, while trying to corral my small runaway, I was shattered, but raring to go and get in among the music. After a fun few hours exploring, playing giant marimbas, beating on bongos and dancing wildly in the kiddies' area, and just luxuriating in all the sights, sounds and smells, I carried an exhausted boy back to the tent.

With him asleep beside me, I lay listening to the distant, but still brilliant, sound of The Proclaimers on the main stage. Their infectious songs carried on the evening breeze as I snuggled down, so happy to be there, and drifted off with an overwhelming feeling that this festival really was something special.

When my wee lad's night nappy leaked and drenched his sleeping bag, he woke, cold and crying, at 6.00 am. Removing his soggy pyjamas, I took him into my bag, hoping cosiness would lull him back to sleep, but it didn't work. There was nothing for it but to drive the fourteen miles home, make hot porridge and toast, get a warm bath and a change of clothes, and then trundle back to Belladrum in time for noon kick-off.

The rest of the day was spent with my son's best friend from Gaelic playgroup, and, with heavy rain having drenched the site, they had hours of fun, splatting and welly-sliding in the mud. I did no cooking, we used none of the food or toys, and it all had to be lugged back to the car along with a sodden but very happy toddler. Maybe I didn't get to see as many bands as I would have liked but it didn't matter; the vibe was terrific, it felt safe and family-friendly, and everyone was in great form and obviously having the best fun. We were hooked.

Since then we have missed the festival just once, when Bruce's sister got married on that August weekend. However, from the stunning wedding venue of Achnagairn House in Kirkhill we could see the end-of-festival fireworks, so still felt we had managed a wee connection. We've seen so many favourite bands, discovered new ones and forged many lasting friendships. Bursting with talent, entertainment and activities for all ages, every year it somehow manages to get better, with quirky new happenings in unexpected corners, while still retaining its magical 'enchanted garden' feel.

Twelve years on from our initial festival experience, my teenager and I now go with band and friends in a convoy of caravans and campervans. My bones and joints no longer appreciate sleeping on hard ground, and a wee touch of home comfort makes all the difference when you've got a gig to do. With food stalls offering just the kind of hearty fare needed to see us through the weekend, I still don't bother with much cooking. A large entourage of youngsters, consisting of Dorec-a-belle children and their chums, hang out together, look out for each other and even come to dance down at the front when we're onstage.

Happily, my son's musical journey continues with the piano and bagpipes. There are very few experiences more heart-stoppingly beautiful than playing music with your child, and we love duetting on piano and accordion or pipes and piano (it's pleasantly surprising how well those two instruments sound together). Although his heart is set more on professional football than music, the carting of camping gear back and forth over many years was worth every frayed muscle as the experiences have helped instil a deep appreciation of the fun to be had in playing, collaborating and enjoying all kinds of music, especially with others. If only I could still get him to wear wellington boots for mud-sliding – the pristine white trainers he favours for festivals nowadays don't quite fit the bill.

The power of a song

With another fabulous Loopallu marking the end of our summer Highland festivals, autumn seems to have brushed lightly in the door, right on cue. Colouring trees with brilliant flashes of scarlet and gold, and yellowing our plants and hedgerows, Nature once again reminds us of her constancy, her reliable cycles of change which, as we might say, keep the whole show on the road. Even the still-hot, low sun of the afternoon has a clarity and freshness – unlike drowsy, dry summer – offering subtle hints of chilled air and frost to come.

Nature's cycles are especially welcome and comforting, not only because of their bountiful beauty and wonder, but because we humankind seem to be stuck relentlessly in a worn-out groove of same-old scourges of conflict, hypocrisy, greed and intransigence. The West and Russia are back at loggerheads, thousands of people are still on the move across Europe and Africa, fleeing violence and barbarity in their homelands, homelessness and poverty have hit record high levels around the world, more lives are devastated by the latest terrorist or gun carnage, lies, abuse and corruption in high places are revealed every week and rich politicians force austerity on the rest of us.

Many of the dystopian visions of Aldous Huxley's 1932 *Brave New World* no longer seem so alien; already we have, for example, corporate tyranny, behavioural conditioning and rampant consumption. Deals are being done behind closed doors, in the stealthy guise of 'Trade Partnership Agreements', which really mean a big-business free-for-all, where profit rules and all public services are up for grabs. The accepted economic mantra of the need for ever-increasing growth goes unchallenged, despite putting our environment and other species sharing this planet under severe pressure and very nearly to tipping-point.

Even in the twenty-first century, we humans still haven't found ways of living in peace and harmony, devised structures of governance, service provision and production to meet the needs of all, or created the conditions in which all people can live joyfully, contentedly and to their full potential, instead of simply struggling for survival. It seems we remain lunatics in charge of the asylum, and if more evidence were needed, reflect on the schoolboy exchanges of certain powerful leaders, putting the world at risk with loose name-calling and rhetoric, or the infantile 'Go away and shut up'-level of diplomacy of the man charged with the UK government's defence portfolio. Burns observed:

O wad some Pow'r the giftie gie us
To see oursels as ithers see us!
It wad frae mony a blunder free us[*]

If there is intelligent life out there in the universe, what in the name of goodness would they make of us?

It is all too easy to catalogue mankind's barbarism, inequalities and general madness around the world – despite this, I remain a glass-half-full optimist. I freely admit to hippy tendencies and firmly believe in the potential for change; who knows, maybe even an Age of Aquarius. For every major human blunder, there are many more small examples of goodness and hope, and nowhere is the examination of the human condition and striving for change more evident than in the arts.

Writers, artists, dramatists, poets and musicians down the ages have always discussed, reflected, satirised and critiqued their times. Indeed, is that not the function of art? Bruce Springsteen once said he learned more from a three-minute song than he ever did in school. Down the centuries, from the ballads of the Diggers and Levellers, through to the nineteenth-century songs of Isle of Skye poet Mary MacPherson (Màiri Mhòr nan Oran[†]) decrying the injustices and persecution of the Highland Clearances, to the global influence of Woody Guthrie, Bob Dylan and Pete Seeger's output – to name but a few – the power of song should not be underestimated.

---

[*]   If only some power would gift us the ability to see ourselves as others see us, it might free us from so many mistakes. From the poem *To a Louse*, by Robert Burns.

[†]   Big Mary of the songs (Gaelic)

I was involved in a day of music not long ago at Dingwall's Greenhouse venue, where songwriters and musicians gathered as part of a country-wide 'We Shall Overcome' movement – a cultural stand against austerity politics and its resulting fall-out. Local music promoter Rob Ellen explained:

In our communities, people are being hit hard by home-lessness and poverty. There is human cost to the politics of austerity. Let's do what we do but let's do it under the one unified banner – We Shall Overcome.

He, like the other organisers, recognises the benefit of galvanising local artistes to sing out on behalf of those who often feel they have no voice, about issues badly affecting those who already have least.

Stuart Maconie, writer and Radio 6 Music broadcaster, laments the lack of modern songwriters tackling a range of subjects, as past generations did:

There used to be records about other things than the personal life of the singers. You used to get people writing about politics or class or the countryside. I don't see any songs about that any more. Maybe folk singers are writing about big subjects, but there was a time when big bands like The Beatles, The Clash or The Smiths wrote about more than their personal circumstances. I think songs have become slightly more banal in what they are about over the last decade.

He has a good point, one with which I would largely concur regarding the pop world. In the folk arena it's different, and with artistes including Davy Cowan, Hamish MacDonald, Sara Bills, Pat Shez, and Conor O'Hara taking part in our local event, there was nothing banal about the songs being sung there. There was passion, wisdom, insight, poignancy and messages aplenty, in song and spoken-word contributions that explored many big and challenging subjects.

For myself, I gave mind, body and soul a treat by taking a countryside walk in that rejuvenating autumn sunshine, and afterwards I topped up nature's boost at the Greenhouse with those wonderful songs-for-change from some of the Highlands' top writers. With a feel-good battery charge like that, we *shall* overcome.

The album launch

What is it about a launch? You invariably spend months carefully planning every detail to create what you hope will be the most entertaining, smooth-running and unforgettable event ever: choosing exactly the right wording for invitations; budgeting; discussing food and drink options; having briefings with the venue manager; scheduling the running-order; and eagerly daydreaming about crowd management issues.

And, of course, trying on everything in the wardrobe in search of something that still fits, keeping front of mind that nightmare concert when tiny nails in my accordion's casing snagged the lace of my dress, preventing the bellows – the bit that creates the sound – from opening. Note to self: nothing fiddly that might trap me in my own unwanted Houdini moment, or too short, causing it to roll up under the movement of the accordion, as my sister helpfully flagged up for me once during a gig. Gesticulating wildly at me from in front of the stage, I had no idea what she meant, but she certainly succeeded in being highly distracting.

All this to present your product, which itself will

be the culmination of years of study, application and the investment of energy and resources, and of course those thousands of hours of practice. You strive to create that conducive ambience in which your audience will feel relaxed and comfortable, and therefore receptive to your presentation, because it's not only a celebration – you do hope to sell some stuff, too. Although it's a given that you be reasonably competent in your craft before you foist your work on the public, it seems you must also be something of a psychologist to get it all right.

Perhaps unsurprising then, with so much to remember, that something invariably gets forgotten on the night. Or is it just me? I am, after all, someone who has spent hours labouring over a hot stove for a party, rustling up pots of thick, nourishing soup or chilli – comfort food to revive the most ardent imbiber in the early hours – only to quaff a couple of glasses of wine and completely forget to serve it up to the revellers.

At our wedding in 1999, I arranged for the cake to be decorated with the music of a lovely slow air composed by my husband-to-be. The baker's handiwork was nothing short of stunning, with the musical notation so delicately rendered it seemed criminal to cut into it. However, it turned out no crime was committed because cutting the cake was exactly what we forgot to do. The more I must remember, the more likely I am to forget something crucial.

In the weeks running up to the launch of our debut album, we women of Dorec-a-belle were up to our ears in preparations, drawing everything together for the big night. It was the culmination of several years of writing, rehearsing and gigging, not to mention endless hours of those other two integral pillars of a musician's life – lugging heavy instruments around and hanging about at soundchecks. With a hunch that my tendency to forgetfulness might let me down I was leaving nothing to chance, and so ten minutes before doors opened my bandmates found me feverishly scribbling amid a flurry of pieces of paper.

'What on earth are you doing?' they laughed.

'Just in case I forget what to say,' I explained, as I accidentally brushed half my notes to the floor with my elbow. Scrabbling to gather them up and put them back in the right order, I realised I couldn't read my own scrawling handwriting without my glasses, so then a hunt for said spectacles. I was just sifting through the fiddly scraps of paper when the first guests began drifting into the function room. Early. 'But I've still got stuff to write – they can't be here yet!' A panic button pinged in my brain, unleashing a disturbed ants' nest of checklists, running orders, jokes and song lyrics. With so much to remember …

It was a fantastic night: friends, family and supporters packed the Glen Mhòr Hotel's function room; the bubbly slipped down a treat; we remembered to cut the specially made cake with the cover photo of our album iced on top; we waved to the National Mod's magical torchlight procession as it weaved its way along the opposite bank of the River Ness; folk had a chuckle at the slideshow of the Dorec-a-belle story, with our many memorable, if not always flattering, moments; and we played a selection of songs from the album and sold a load of CDs.

And, yes, of course I forgot a variety of essentials, including thanking three of the most vital people there. Robin Abbot, our double bass player, and Derek Urquhart on drums have brought, with their immense talent and sympathetic, intuitive musicianship, yet more richly textured layers to the Dorec-a-belle sound, as well as wonderfully driving, meaty power when needed. John Aitken on the mixing desk did his usual skilful job, creating a warm, clear mix onstage and making us sound great out front. Miss Forgetful strikes again.

Other people's worlds

One of my semi-regular gigs is playing the piano for a family that owns an extensive sporting estate, who fly in on a private jet from their Scandinavian home perhaps a dozen times a year. Their Highland hideaway is a substantial, secluded mansion, nestling among tall, mature trees in magnificent grounds. Surrounded by hills and fronted by an immaculate, vast lawn, it surely comprises one of the most superb locations in Scotland.

The house interior has been modernised, and exudes comfort and relaxed, understated luxury. Being also, as far as I can see, free of television and other electronic gadgets, it offers the family and their visitors the perfect getaway from the pressures of busy lives and work. Guests include friends, business colleagues and members of their country's government and royalty, and, while days are spent on the hills in all weathers, their evenings are enjoyed in convivial relaxation. A private chef and waiting staff are brought in for the night to prepare a sumptuous meal, overseeing with orderly calm each minute detail of the meticulous table settings and attending to every need throughout the evening.

My role is to contribute to the ambience with background music, which, as I appreciate from years of playing in restaurants and hotels, is about treading a fine line of judgement. Nothing loud or intrusive but, rather, soothing and mellow with glints of light and shine, engaging enough to offer interest and sparkle during lapses in dinner conversation. Easy listening does not have to mean bland and, while always mindful that this gig is not a concert demanding audience attention, I'm careful to choose a repertoire that offers variety in tempo, feel and style. As the family and guests dress for dinner upstairs, I get myself organised at the piano.

I invariably move the stuffed grouse sideways a little on the lid, so he isn't eyeballing me quite so directly. Various two- and formerly four-legged shooting 'trophies' stare from their perches, and although their wild lives were cut short by some other, I can't look them in the eye. I know they long to wrench themselves free from their wooden plinths and take to the hills, and I wish I could help. The male black grouse is a beauty, his scarlet wattle vivid and striking, the tilt of his neat head suggesting he was a fine specimen, cutting a dash in the grouse world. Shot in his prime for sport, I feel the accusation in his sharp, beady eye and block his sideways gaze with sheet music.

It often puzzles us Scots why so many other nationalities love our traditional heritage to such a great extent and, indeed, embrace our music, songs, history and language with a dedication that can put us to shame in our own, at times deficient, knowledge or appreciation. Many Scottish folk bands make much of their livelihood touring abroad, such is the love of our music among Europeans and North Americans, and many such fans even settle in Scotland for the sole purpose of learning Gaelic and being closer to our traditional music.

I've attended numerous workshops where learning a tune elicited discussion on the so-called 'correct' version and possible alternatives. It is invariably the individual from southerly Sussex or faraway San Francisco, with no personal connection to Scotland, who can enlighten the class as to whether a certain note should be, for instance, an E or an E flat, according to *The Skye Collection* or any number of other music books. In contemplating their admirable depth of study and knowledge, I ponder whether it's the dissipation and dearth of their own culture that moves them to connect so deeply with ours.

So it is with the visiting Scandinavians. They love Scottish music, particularly airs and ballads, and are loyal followers of Runrig, to whose *Loch Lomond* they can sing along, word perfect. Their passion for Scotland is warm and enthusiastic, and adopting the role of laird* is an appealing element of what they perceive as Scottish-ness. Coming downstairs for dinner, the family wear smart kilt dress in their own estate tartan. They have bought into Scotland literally, lock, stock and barrel.

I am usually asked to play in late autumn, during pheasant- and stag-shooting season, when it's dark by the time I arrive. As I turn off the main road and down the driveway, lighted windows and the orange

---

*   landowner/lord (Scots)

glow of exterior lights against the house offer an inviting welcome through black trees and bushes. I immediately anticipate the warmth inside, the aroma of good food cooking and the evening ahead. It feels as if I am about to leave my world and enter a parallel universe where everything is beautiful, luxurious, perfect. As my car tyres crunch to a halt on the stones and I ready myself for stepping into this other arena, as an entertainer, an outsider, I am reminded of my first awareness of this same feeling.

For part of my early schooling, I attended a small rural primary school in Farr, near Inverness, where one teacher taught all twenty children in a single classroom. It was a lesson in the curios of a forgotten age. Walls were still hung with vast, shiny maps emblazoning Empire pink across the known world, and ancient, all-in-one wooden desks gripped us tight between lid and seat as we chanted Britain's imperial measures – 'ten chains one furlong, eight furlongs one mile' – and recited old words that seemed to belong to a bygone age: *pecks, bushels, roods.*

My close friend there, before she was dispatched to boarding school, was the daughter of a local estate owner. A clan chief with additional Highland estates, a yacht in the Mediterranean and diverse interests elsewhere, he was lord of a modern mock castle perched on the shoulder of the craggy slope where his forebears had, for centuries, presided over their dominion. My friend's mother, a kindly, gentle and quite beautiful woman, occasionally invited me over to play the baby grand piano in their drawing room.

This aristocratic family listened attentively as I

played a selection of pieces, my gaze furtively wandering to pictures and through large windows to the expansive view down the glen. I felt rather like a performing monkey, scoffing down the cake and sweet rewards which followed those little recitals with a relish and haste, as if I hadn't eaten for days. Although it all felt somewhat embarrassing, I deemed it worth it for the sake of the goodies and the fact that afterwards my friend and I would sneak upstairs to the bedroom of their young help, raid her underwear drawer and try on her bras.

The nanny's brassieres, which we padded generously with tissues, held much greater fascination for me at age eleven than the baby grand, but what I was beginning to learn, and which has been reinforced many times since, is that music will take you into other people's unfamiliar worlds if you let it, and what you find there, or what you make of it, can be an adventure in itself.

Paris: memories of a magnificent city

The sun was up past the yardarm of bulbous blue pipes of the Pompidou Centre, flooding the square with light and the promise of another sweltering day. My boyfriend patted the velvet bag of his bagpipes into life – two-handed as if plumping a cushion – his right cheek bulging like a ripe plum, eyes fixed ahead. The first phlegmy wheeze dragged itself up to a reluctant, drowsy drawl, and, fingering each drone in turn, he held the rod of sound steady until he got the true tone he was after. He adjusted the bag wedged under his left arm and launched into a tune.

Heads turned, and folk started to drift over for a closer look. He was soon sweating under the weight of his kilt, but it was worth it, because no squad of fire-eaters, sword-swallowers, bed-of-nails guys or lean, circus types wearing nothing but chains and loincloths can compete with a handsome young Scotsman in a kilt playing the pipes. Other buskers, from all over the world and each with an identikit rendition of 'American Pie', didn't get a look-in.

The heat put the pipes so far out of tune that we couldn't play together, so I sat on the up-ended accordion case, happy to people-watch and study the bizarre weave of external pipework on this intriguing, inside-out arts centre. After fifteen minutes and many photographs I took my turn to go through my repertoire – luckily the audience was transient, and I could repeat tunes without anyone being any the wiser. We had heard that Paris empties in August, but it seemed busy and passers-by were generous. After two or three hours, sweaty, slippery fingers and exhaustion from the stifling blanket of afternoon heat made it impossible to play any longer, so we packed up, strapped the accordion onto my little shopping trolley and rumbled back through the teeming streets to our hotel.

This was my first day in Paris. My paternal grandfather, once a jazz band pianist on trans-Atlantic liners in the 1920s, had told me long ago, 'If you can play music, you'll never starve,' and he was right, for there I was earning my bed and board by playing the accordion on the streets of Paris: the city of art, music and revolution; city of the young Hemingway, Picasso and Piaf; streets walked by some of the greatest writers and philosophers, and the Impressionists; and its cafes frequented by Sartre and de Beauvoir.

It was 1982 and my first time abroad. With return bus tickets safely stored with our newly acquired British visitors' passports (no budget airlines in those days), the world, as my Glaswegian boyfriend laughingly proclaimed, was our oxter.* As an idealistic, twenty-one-year-old dreamer, recently graduated from Glasgow

---

*   armpit (Scots)

University, I felt on top of the world. Everything about Paris was intoxicatingly exciting and exotic: being served *café au lait* at pavement tables by neat, white-aproned waiters; patisserie windows engorged with sticky, golden delights; the effortless chic of Parisians who possessed such a dignified, self-assured style; the art-nouveau-embellished Metro signs; the footprints of history on every boulevard.

During our two weeks there we established something of a routine, busking for a few hours in the morning then exploring the city until foot-weary. Some afternoons we braved the queues at the Louvre or Eiffel Tower or wandered in the Tuileries Garden to get a fix of greenery and escape crowds and traffic. When it got too hot we took refuge in the cool of a bar with a well-earned beer then followed our noses to find a small family-run, backstreet restaurant, where boeuf bourguignon would invariably be delicious and the house red extremely palatable, all served on quintessential red-checked tablecloths. Later, we might retire to a music bar, one of our favourite haunts being The Silver Goblet in Les Halles, which hosted Irish and local musicians and thronged nightly with a young, arty crowd.

Paris left its indelible mark: so much about it has stayed with me, those first exotic impressions imprinting themselves deep on my heart and mind. I have been back several times since then, with music and on holiday, and each visit has served to underline how inimitable the French capital and its people are. Inevitably, every large city also has, unfortunately, its poverty, its underbelly of seediness and criminality and those on the margins of society, and Paris is no different.

However, as a mere wandering minstrel I had the opportunity to revel in the exhilaration of playing for my supper on the streets of that historic city, to soak up its atmosphere, its *je ne sais quoi*, and I'm very thankful for it. Playing at being Bohemian, perhaps, but they were youthful, heady days and I loved every minute. It's no coincidence that the French phrase, *joie de vivre*, is one that has found a home across the world – it perfectly sums up sparkle and vitality, the buoyant feeling that *life is good*, which was what filled my head and heart during that first continental adventure.

For onlookers, and particularly those who have been fortunate to experience the vibrancy, exuberance and romance of Paris, the horrific terrorist attacks unleashed on the city in recent years are not just unspeakably grotesque but they have also left us profoundly saddened and dismayed. Many words have been written about the massacres, far more erudite than mine could ever be, but one of the aspects I find so repugnant is that the targets were places where people gathered to socialise, to listen to music, eat, drink and watch sport – to experience the communal enjoyment of life.

When I saw the online video of the man wheeling his piano to the Bataclan and playing John Lennon's 'Imagine', I thought of the old Gaelic proverb, *Mairidh gaol is ceol* – love and music will endure. The pianist was spot-on; without words or fuss he simply sat down and played what was without doubt the most appropriate song for that moment, proving, if it needed proving, that music brings people together and touches something in the core of our being that is life-affirming and joyful. Love and music *will* endure and, with them, *joie de vivre*.

Harmony heaven plus a bucket of seaweed

One Direction may have swept the boards at the 2014 MTV Awards in Glasgow, but for us in the Highlands (those of us out of our teens, at least) there is only one vocal-harmony boy band on our musical radar. Winning hearts and plaudits alike, our very own Inverness-based Trosg are rapidly forging a strong profile and loyal following at regular venue and festival gigs, where they not only produce harmonies to die for and sing bluegrass classics in Gaelic, but do it with utterly inimitable style, crack and panache.

The lads – and I'm sure they won't mind me pointing out that I use that word somewhat loosely – are all stalwarts of Inverness Gaelic Choir and include among their number Angus Macleod, whose beguiling and mellifluous voice won him the National Mod's Men's Gold Medal. However, steeped to the gills as they are in the world of competitive singing, they have now branched out to take their considerable talents and love of harmony to a wider audience, and are we glad they did.

When they invited us girls (and I indulge in this appellation equally loosely) in Dorec-a-belle to join them at a November gig, we pounced at the chance. Harmony singing is one of the pivotal passions in our band, and we love nothing more than getting some tasty four-parters on the go – six, if Derek and Robin are with us on drums and double bass – so the thought of hooking up with a ready-made, male-voice ensemble had us drooling at the thought.

I had bumped into Iain Ross, an old friend from university days and founding member of Trosg, and I was keen to find out the meaning of the band name. Despite many childhood summers spent with grand-parents on the Hebridean island of Lewis, I couldn't recall the Gaelic word, *trosg*. 'It means cod,' he explained. 'We only sing songs about fish.'

That's neat, I thought. Gaels are very partial to fish, so that's a sizeable niche market they've got sewn up there. The fact they were playing Belladrum's Walled Garden Free Range Stage, which that year was re-designed as an upturned boat, was not only perfectly appropriate, but surely a PR dream?

When the invitation to collaborate came in, the logistics of there being lots of them and quite a few of us meant we did not manage a full rehearsal but just a quick get-together of some of us to run a couple of songs by each other and try a few wee harmony possibilities. We learned that the boys had cast their net wider since Belladrum to include songs of the sea and indeed other subject matter, and as they launched into 'I'll Fly Away' – a 1929 hymn that later became a gospel and bluegrass standard – we sat in stunned silence as their rich bass sound filled the room. Smiles swept our faces; this was going be good.

While the show itself is possibly best described as more crack than slick, it was possibly the most fun I've had at a gig. The songs went surprisingly well, given the lack of rehearsal, and it was awesome, in the true sense of the word, to hear Trosg's deep, treacle tones fill out the bottom end, as we say in the trade, of our songs, 'Don't Give Up' and 'Antonia'. From warm, clear tenors down to a Paul Robeson-like bass, their wall of sound, like the thrumming hum of an orchestra, had our skin tingling and rashed with goosebumps. Their Gaelic reworking of Tom Jones's 'Delilah' – 'Dolina' – was sheer genius.

What came next, however, perfectly rounded off this musical treat. As at all self-respecting Highland events there was a raffle, and the array of intriguing prizes hinted strongly at the island lineage of Trosg members, not to say some would-be mariners among them: a half bottle of Navy Rum, a whole mackerel, a home-grown parsnip and copies of two staples of my grandparents' house, *The People's Friend* and *The Stornoway Gazette*, the front-page headline reading, 'Lewis man sails to ends of earth to break world record'.

As I was musing on the Flat Earth Society being yet alive and twitching, I realised my ticket was drawn and got handed my prize. I instantly recognised it as eminently superior booty: a bucket of dried seaweed. On childhood holidays our mother identified for my siblings and me the edible *dulaisg* on the shore, expounding on its nutritional value, and we never left Lewis without a pail of seaweed for use in her bath, its miraculous properties being equally beneficial to skin.

Harvested, dried and milled on the island of South Uist, the seaweed meal is top-notch stuff. Iain explained it is sold as a mineral garden fertiliser and livestock feed supplement, and it's so highly regarded that Arab sheikhs import it for their thoroughbred racehorses. Levering off the lid, the evocative and unmistakable tang of the sea had me at once back to carefree summer days in my grandmother's village of Calbost, beach-combing my way across the endless slippery rocks of the *cladach.** It was a fitting end to an immensely enjoyable evening.

We took our leave with promises to sing together again and, bowled over as we were by Trosg's heavenly harmonies, we're certain that these boys have not only the smell of the sea in their nostrils but also the scent of success. Now, where did I put that bucket? If it's good for racehorses, then how better to turn back the tide of the years ... I'm off to sprinkle some on my porridge.

---

*   stony beach (Scottish Gaelic)

The office party

It's December and so, of course, it's the Scots Trad Music Awards. If anything reflects more singularly how Scotland's cultural landscape has matured and grown in confidence in recent years it's the Trads, whose home on the folk calendar is now well-established in the first weekend of the month.

Having recently enjoyed its fifteenth outing, this magnificent, moveable feast has developed, in every sense, since its founding by Simon Thoumire and his Hands Up for Trad organisation in 2003. A celebration of some of the best in traditional music, it has blossomed into a glitzy evening of sparkly gowns, tuxedos and champagne, where our musicians and those working to promote the music are hailed and honoured for their contribution to our nation's cultural life.

With nominations open to all and winners chosen by public vote from shortlisted entries, the categories are numerous, from Composer, Live Act, Gaelic Singer and Pipe Band of the Year, to Scots Singer, Event, Folk Club and Tutor of the Year. It's especially good to see projects be recognised for innovation, originality or educational reach, as well as young bands like Elephant Sessions achieve an astonishingly successful trajectory, from winning the Up and Coming Act Award to Album of the Year in just three years. To underline the calibre of talent from which nominees have been shortlisted, showcase spots from a diverse range of bands, solo artistes and ensembles, whose abilities, musicianship and performances are invariably outstanding, are interspersed throughout the evening.

Musicians, of course, don't function in isolation; also enjoying the revels are those who work with us all year round in the fields of promotion, agency and management, festival organisation, media, technical expertise, CD production and the myriad other areas vital to maintaining the infrastructure necessary for a sustainable and professional folk music industry. Many awards are sponsored by those same organisations, labels, funding bodies and music associations, further testament to the commitment of numerous individuals and agencies to backing this prestigious occasion and the world of traditional music.

Supported by the Gaelic media service, MG Alba, and broadcast live on the Gaelic television channel, BBC Alba, online and on BBC Radio Scotland, 'Na Trads' is one of several relatively new annual award events celebrating the arts and cultural sectors. Recognition that Scotland's creative industries now make such a substantial contribution to the economy, as well as the richness of lives, is heartening and reinforces the notion, for those who don't believe us, that we do, after all, have a proper job. In straitened times of cuts and austerity, it is a message that is more important than ever to get across to the powers-that-be, as music and the arts are often the first victims of the axe.

The gathering, hosted in a different city each year, is one of fun, bonhomie and camaraderie, and as most folkies seem to possess a natural penchant for letting their hair down on any excuse, the chance to catch up with friends, carouse and kick up our high heels is grasped eagerly. Long gone is the clichéd image of the bearded folk singer in a big woolly jumper with a finger in his ear – these days you are more likely to see sharply dressed young fellas – yes, beards are still *in*, but these new ones are carefully groomed and coiffured – and radiant women resplendent in beautiful finery. The 'Oscars of the Scottish folk world' are a glittering and glamorous affair, but the genuine affection in which the event and its organiser are held is evident in the social media hashtag which has sprung up around it – #folkiesofficeparty. A perfect description.

Simon's Hands Up for Trad has grown many arms and legs over the last decade, developing numerous projects and initiatives, using new technologies to facilitate and build infrastructure that increases the profile and visibility of Scottish traditional music. His sterling work is appreciated and valued by all in the folk world, and this now-iconic pillar of our community, the Trad Awards, is important in recognising not just current musical achievement but also significant contribution in a wider cultural sense. Awarding Services to Gaelic and Scots, Lifetime Achievement and Hall of Fame inductees, they acknowledge a bigger picture: one of connection, identity, collaboration and great heart.

We are fortunate to have many passionate and

inspirational cultural ambassadors, who have made it their life's work to promote, play, sing, teach, mak,* nurture and hand on our Scottish folk heritage and languages to a new generation. In his acceptance speech for Services to Scots at the Awards in 2016, writer and broadcaster Billy Kay asked:

> *Hou can ye be fully yersel gin ye bide*
> *ignorant o the cultural tradeitions that hae*
> *wrocht ye ower hunners o years?*†

There is, without doubt, much work still to be done, but that our year is book-ended by two such superb events – Celtic Connections launching gloriously in January with an energising tsunami of music and The Trads ushering forth winter and the run-up to Christmas and Hogmanay, with year-end reflection and celebration of the previous twelve months – affirms how far things have come in the maturing folk scene.

Billy went on to quote one of Scotland's greatest poets, Hugh MacDiarmid:

> *Tae be yersels an tae mak that worth bein, nae*
> *harder job tae mortals has been gien.*‡

---

* make/write/compose (Scots)
† How can you be fully yourself if you live in ignorance of the cultural traditions which have affected you / created you over the centuries? (Scots)
‡ To be yourselves and to make that worth being, there's been no harder job given to mortals. (Scots)

To be ourselves, comfortable and at ease and confident in our own cultural skin; to value who and what we came from; to appreciate our folk heritage and how it can sustain us, bring meaning and nourish our souls. And venture forward with it in whatever exciting and inspiring ways it moves us. That, for me, is the nub of it.

Note on the author

Liza Mulholland is from Inverness in the Highlands of Scotland. She studied Scottish History and Sociology at the University of Glasgow before going on to work as a musician, playing across Britain, Ireland and mainland Europe. For several years she also devised and produced TV and radio arts documentaries for BBC Scotland in her independent production company, Metagama Productions.

Taking time out in 2004 to set up and run the family's outdoor activities and events business at Bogbain Farm, Inverness, she returned to full-time music in 2011. She has played on over a dozen albums and released her debut self-penned, solo album, Fine 'n' Rosy, in 2016. Her feature writing has been published in newspapers and journals. *Notes from a Scottish musician's year* is the first book in her *Inside Folk* series. She lives in her home town with her son and two cats.

www.lizamulholland.com

Acknowledgements

My gratitude goes to numerous friends and colleagues who have encouraged and assisted in many ways, including my Inverness writing 'families' in the Highland Literary Salon, SCBWI community, Ness Book Fest and Emergents. Fine company and camaraderie play a big part in helping keep on keepin' on. Special thanks go to Barbara Henderson, who kindly read through the manuscript and offered many wise suggestions.

To writer and broadcaster Billy Kay, and Monica Neeling, director of Artsplay Highland, my sincere thanks and appreciation for such thoughtful feedback and generous reviews. For Simon Thoumire's foreword, imbued with the trademark enthusiasm that colours everything he does in Hands Up for Trad, my deep gratitude – you truly are an inspiration. Warm thanks also to Martin Hadden of Birnam CD for reading an early draft, taking the time to discuss particular points and making many helpful recommendations.

Without the team at *The Highland Times*, who first featured some of my music writing in a column over a period of two years, this *Inside Folk* series might never have happened; I appreciate having had that opportunity. Grateful thanks also to my editor, Denise Cowle, for her invaluable input and advice.

My music 'family' over several decades is truly special. There is no bond quite like that forged by playing music together, and my heartfelt thanks go to all the musicians with whom I've had the privilege of enjoying so much fun, fraternity and friendship. Warmest gratitude to my soul sisters and misters in our band, Dorec-a-belle, with whom I enjoy the most exciting music and the best of times.

My son, Roddy MacGregor, has witnessed this project evolve over many months and has patiently and consistently bolstered my resolve with his words of encouragement and confidence; to you, my deepest love and thanks.

Lightning Source UK Ltd.
Milton Keynes UK
UKHW02f2135100718
325520UK00007B/333/P